OBEDIENT LAUGHTER

OBEDIENT LAUGHTER

OBEDIENT *Laughter*

Ray DiPalma

OTIS BOOKS | SEISMICITY EDITIONS

The Graduate Writing program
Otis College of Art and Design
LOS ANGELES ● 2014

"Agora" and "Salt Plumes" originally appeared in *Verse*. "After Midnight" was first published in the *Chicago Review*. To the editors of these journals the author extends his grateful acknowledgment.

Book design and typesetting: Rebecca Chamlee

ISBN-13: 978-0-9860173-3-9
ISBN: 0-9860173-3-7

OTIS BOOKS | SEISMICITY EDITIONS
The Graduate Writing program
Otis College of Art and Design
9045 Lincoln Boulevard
Los Angeles, CA 90045

https://blogs.otis.edu/seismicity
http://gw.otis.edu
seismicity@otis.edu

TABLE *of* CONTENTS

AFTER MIDNIGHT

for Merrill Gilfillan

Two-headed monsters, ghouls, torrents of human blood,
and fearful astronomical happenings

Brasses, charcoal drawings, carvings in ivory and wood,
fireworks, burning hair, chloroform, banknotes

Brown rabbits, tailor's dummies, photographs, calipers,
rubber stamps, dismantled cameras, postcards

Boxes of matches, half-smoked cigars, fountain pens,
bottles of ink and glue, tubes of oil paint, lighter fluid

Partially filled notebooks, a stopwatch,
green candles, a Chinese screen, knives and forks

Battered shoes, rolls of black electrical tape, a flashlight,
small stacks of cardboard, dead light bulbs, a scalpel

A scattering of costume jewelry, a tin whistle, a hammer,
a deck of cards missing the aces, a hand mirror, a radio

*

The details depend on who's telling the story,
a quay in a forgotten city, three archival folders

The peripatetic game we pass through, moving silently away,
the quarry beyond the olive grove, the vineyards spoiled by a
    frost in late May

Stacks of letters, ill-starred commercial ventures,
a line length equivalent to three strides across a balcony

Sequestered in a displacement provisionally assumed,
detached details lurking in potential ambush

Hidden political meaning in the mode of dress,
scientific procedures, control of strategic territory

Topography and poetics, the inflection of a few dactyls,
a severance, solitude, scenarios, under a Mediterranean sky

Preparatory fragments described in retrospect,
the very name of the place a few yards beyond the body

*

Without a fixed destination, as a matter of form,
bargaining notations, mnemonic targets, omertà

A third signature, distraction's forward gaze,
pale abbreviations, the limits of a compass turn

Assertion is within the exclusion and without the inclusion,
I can remember neither the lament it prompted nor its novelty

There are no false alarms, no after-effects honorably offered,
no obscure etymologies, arias, no discernible debt

A type font peculiar to negotiations, constant measurement,
a block of salt, spilled shapes, blank inlays, a German wife

Rain shadows, red seeds, the heft of blue serge,
no want of material display, the game continues

Misled by thought, refractive, invisible commotion, eye for one,
only panorama, muled from place to place, interrogated

*

Calm assurance, disappearance, 2 then 3 tempered by scrutiny,
some possibly all, else are surrounding pools, trees, broken
   statues

No description, vertices, rational, tolerant, serene,
an elaborate edge reflected in surface, newness, newness

Nine stones, pi's torsion, even if suggests memory, repeated
    tangents,
remembered out of their frames, 2 drifting into a 3rd

The bird flies the angle it has been given to see who is coming,
mathematics released from the things it realizes, a contradiction
    of lights

Fear mating the calm and gray with eagerness,
see nothing, taste nothing, say nothing, turned to stone

Contenting synonyms, contesting libraries, making do,
bare methods the further product of an instance

Quills, spiders, weeds, sunlight, domes, congruent expansions,
a spectrum, white not absence behind the whole thing

*

A lot of people in your position, set in the distance comparable to
    exclusion,
see the dialogue as a series of half-triumphs

The word shows a little archaic, singing, dancing, playing
    instruments,
you read what has been liberated, what has been puzzled out of
    spare formalities

Better now than in the Sunday papers, spoken for the first time,
in the noise of changing songs and dialects, the new pause

The distance from the thunder to the lightning, sealed in the reply,
serves as a reasonable substitute, an upturned glance

All sorts of attractions, nothing guaranteed, open, windy spaces,
the insinuating look of skepticism exhausted by the assurance
    of many secrets

The self which is life, and the self that is not,
long hours about the idea, no thought of ever reaching its goal

Poète courageux, critique courageux, homme courageux,
you are still here, I will restore what belongs to you

*

Influence and speculation reduced to the arguable, the exact
    wording
of the resolution will be worked out by disinterested parties
    for a fee

The sharp edge and smooth surface where you cannot go,
forbearance and its distant purpose bring doubts and watery
    rhythms

The crisis in your fingers and throat,
a white mist hanging over the trees in the park

No, I said, it wasn't an unreasonable hour,
you and I could begin again for the last time

I don't believe this detail figures in any other version,
this detail, it's an evolutionary step, the casualty of a resolution

To say I have retained virtually no memory of it would be to lie,
within as without, provided the latter involves a certain cruelty

Conventional, however grotesque, our heads roll,
according to the degrees of concentration

*

The Dioscuri, italianuccio, this is merely a suggestion,
a subjective impression, there's no way of verifying it

An enchanted island, the hum of shadowy penitents,
a shape that could have resembled anything deprived of repose

A man goes into a room, there are no windows, no doors,
how does he get out—the same way he got in

As many wiles as anticipations, a flirtatious life,
distracted, he whistles, a conversation, putting your face to
    the window

All inner darkness, a malaise of anticipation,
eye mediates eye, audible pleasures born of confinement

Another self, true as an instrument, a departure for a symptom,
or a series of antecedents and sequels, nothing but unmastered
    forms

What mixtures, what diffusions, abstract sensations,
    ceremonies,
reproaches, or only old denials, old supplications

                              *

Just now from that capacious window and its view of the
    pine forest
lit by a small shrewd light in the hall, nails filed under nails

It should be obvious you are now hearing the reach of the wall,
outside: clockwise in the room, inside: counterclockwise from
    the room

One more body one less suspect, you hear the echo,
under a high peaked roof where the animals look for people

An objective analysis reported to the subconscious, music,
can such a thing be, in which I sing can such a thing be

After all means nothing's closer than we thought,
as far as the wall, the ear pressed to the wall, than we thought

A perimeter of contagion, false information, nothing earns
    entry,
at the same time, and at the same time: the light returns

But there is no answer since I am here, better you were,
circling under water, removed from the cited page

*

Ropemates, here's your favorite chair, the lions could care less,
a landscape to be duplicated, a government to be planned,
    words

The maker's signature: I know I should do what I have done
another bottle of wine difficult to open, bring water, bring
    more wine

We are walking from room to room, meeting sound,
or is it music from the radio picking its way through the
    afternoon

Thrown shadows from which I quote: names are the
    consequence of things,
a new riddle without time or honor—pure attribution, etwas
    filzig

The benefit of the doubt comes with suspicious benediction,
this report contains no reliable evidence obtained from
    informants

If I bring a ladder to the window I can see to the south and the
    east,
point-to-point, what is indeterminate begins in the middle
    distance

Bricks, oak beams, cobble, lath, sheets of hammered tin, debris,
the rotating earth translates the view, secures the distance
    necessary

*

On a different level, a deliberate loss of information, mute
    probability,
stepping backwards, as if just awakening, no sense of deferral,
    stunned

The certainty of physical contact burdens every activity, finding
    the words,
in proportion to knowing the words, a category of sequence
    regardless of fact

Failure hinged to privacy hinged to the limits of calculation,
the iconography of the site is a proliferation of rejected
    attainments

Individuals, no empathy, no ethos, but these were attainments,
earned by taking your own or someone else's memory and
    dissolving it in aspiration

Lines of sight merge with an undisclosed context,
    commensurate,
unraveling the heard from the disclosed, the seen from the
    revealed

But from which assumed identity to begin, one sustaining the
    other,
one dividing the other, exposure keeps them aloof

Companions at the shadow's edges, the place of calculations,
no map, no air, no easy way out

August-September, 2003

EQUIVOQUES

Yaahoooo!

—SLIM PICKENS, *DOCTOR STRANGELOVE*

HEGEMONY OF THE CULTURAL FRONTS
Still bringing up the rear.

COLLECTIVE ACTS AND THE QUALITY OF SURVIVAL
Habit protocol learned procedure betrayal.

PREFERABLE DISCLOSURES
Based on patterns of long and short vowels.

FOR NOW
Hear what comes next—it can be read later.

SO THE LEGEND GOES
Seventy rabbis on the Island of Pharos seventy separate versions
    all the same.

FIRST COMBED
First served.

HOW THE SUIT WAS RETURNED
Tionlish tavabic sening cientanin consivarat chovide ascomice.

AN UPHOLSTERED SEWER MASQUERADING AS A NIGHTCLUB
The shadow of your smile.

WHY SOME WOMEN MAKE BETTER SPIES THAN MEN
Knowing you.

IN 1966 THEY HIRED THE COUNT BASIE ORCHESTRA
No one showed up to dance and he died 18 years later.

YOU'RE A TALENTED PERSON AND I'VE SEEN YOU DO THIS BEFORE
For the edification of all please step up your shadow and
    disappear.

CAPTURED BY A SINGLE DIMENSION
Appraisals of the self.

SOCIOTROPIC
He dug up her bones and built a cage.

PSYCHOSIS [SEE *GENETICS*]
A more complex but useless theory of mind.

VALIDITY
Fulfills a purpose but must not be confused with reliability.

AS THOUGHT OCCURS
Microcurrents are detectable in the finger muscles.

CHARACTERS ARE UNWELCOME
Especially if you can only play yourself.

TWO CANADIAN PSYCHIATRISTS
Used a questionnaire to measure self-esteem in psychotic
  patients.

DEPRESSION PARANOIA MANIA HALLUCINATIONS AND DISORDERED
  SPEECH
Do not favor the predictive.

EN ROUTE TO LEE HO FOOK'S
Little old lady got mutilated late last night.

WHEN I DIE
That'll be the day.

RAIMUNDO FURIOSO
Non-affective acute remitting psychosis.

SUFFERED BY MANY BUT NOT ALL
Rapid onset followed by complete recovery.

NO WOMAN NO PRIZE
No, woman, no price.

NO MATTER HOW AGGRESSIVELY UNINTENDED
The self is always the center of all narrative gravity.

A PERFECT ORBIT IS NEVER ACHIEVED
Given the pathway through the visual cortex to the limbic
    system.

I HEARD IT THROUGH THE GRAPEVINE
Perfect symbol for the non-linear, people kept saying.

JUNKYARD DOGS
Now living in the penthouse by the reservoir.

WIT WITTERS WALD
Another shade of pale.

DOCK OF THE BAY
Money for nothing, Hawaiian noises, where are you?

ONLY THE PARANOID SURVIVE #2
There are detectives everywhere—all kinds.

HOMAGE TO BEN JONSON [OR *LIKE THE NEXT GUY*]
Light, I salute thee, but with wounded nerves.

FROM ZERO TO ONE
We continue the long journey.

CHOICE
Always a matter of depths.

THE WORD OPENS LIKE A GRAVE
Reserved taciturn cool to the touch.

LATE WINTER HEADING WEST
A wolf vanishes among the trees.

FRINGE PHENOTYPES
Still crazy after all these years.

WHICH WAY
Which way?

OUT OF PATENT
Prime for reconsideration.

A WHITE SPORT COAT
And a pink potato.

OF HUMAN FORMS
With superhuman powers, he said.

XENOS IME KI ILTHA TORA
I am an immigrant and I just came home.

MANY YEARS PASS
And the question that had already been answered is asked
  again.

OUT OF EGYPT
Into the frying pan.

PRIVATE MORTALITY
Always a matter of depth.

OF HUMAN BLONDAGE
But do the curtains match the rug?

NO PLEASURE GIVEN
No pleasure taken no pleasure given none.

DOGS FOR THE DEAD
'Scuse me, you misunderstood, it's dogs for the *deaf.*

ILLUSION
As the incantatory is to the cumulative.

SACRED AND UNDENIABLE
No, Tom, let's go with *self-evident*.

PEACHES AND HERB
I'd wager they taste terrible.

SCAM SCION
Scansion and scumble soldi pronounced sordi.

HO IMMIGRATO E SONO SOLTANTO TORNATO A CASA
Xenos ime ki iltha tora.

ACADEMIC
You need speed on draw plays to take advantage of the creases.

ED ELLI AVEA DEL CUL FATTO TROMBETTA
No cymbals where none intended.

MISSTAKES
Show how good you are otherwise.

PART OF A LARGER EFFORT TO IMPROVE THE BOTTOM LINE
Hallelujah I'm a bum.

HERE TO THERE THERE TO HERE
To how and back.

HAZELNUT BUTTER WITH WILD MUSHROOMS
The studio pays.

DISTRACTION IS TO ABANDONMENT
What memory is to closure.

MEDIATED OR UNMEDIATED
As tactics are to strategy and nevermore is to soltanto.

CETTE MALADIE DU PERDU
Livre tonique ou il n'est d'ailleurs pas.

MAD VIG
Catch up or you're dead.

SNIPER IN THE HELO
Beans bread butter and blood—put me in, coach.

SPATTER UP
Hope doesn't live here.

CREEPIN' AND WEEPIN'
Just too proud to beg, baby. No no no.

PRIVATE MESSAGE [FOR WCW]
The gingerbread is very spicy.

A LA HIÉRARCHISATION DU TEMPS CHRONOLOGIQUE [EH]
The sound of something like that.

A WOMAN I KNEW
Works hard for the money but where's the money?

OLD BRIGHT SHOES [GAETANO THE ATHEIST]
What did he do for a living?

LEAVING BEHIND AND LEAVING BEHIND A TRAIL OF WORDS
Too damn hard to hang up.

HOW LONG DID YOU SPEND IN BEATTY
Only two or three hours and managed to avoid the tour.

DARK DANGER WITH SOFT CORNERS
After you take the money.

AN IMMIGRANT'S PERSPECTIVE
What did your neighbor Bright Shoes do for a living?

THE COLESLAW END OF THE OPERATION
That's where some of it gets done.

HE HAD SOME ANALYTICAL GENIUS
But who doesn't?

DON'T TEAR YOUR THROAT APART
Just to make your point.

BUT DON'T GET ME WRONG
I wish they all could be hallelujah girls.

WITH A ONEHANDED SWING IN THE LATE INNINGS
He bitch-slapped a slider into a double.

FACING A DEVEREAUX
Means nothing but its music must be recorded.

BLOW OF HEAVY HAMMER AGAINST METAL AND STONE BEING
    INESCABABLE
Must be accepted among and along every point the pedestrian.

WELL WHAT D'Y'KNOW
A lost Rothko no a found one.

TO OR FOR
To is always better.

HOW'S BUSINESS
Where's the paper?

POISED SWORD AND LOAF
How many ill-fitting clothes do you have my boy.

BOVARY STILL THE MOTIVATION
Better be good some are hard to convince.

A DISTANT TONE THAT SPARES ALMOST NO SYMPATHY FOR ANY UNIT
    OF SURVIVAL
You know, dialectic—see what all the talk's about.

GOAT-OLD THAT'S HOW OLD GOAT OLD
Don't mind me there'll be more of that too and very soon.

THE DEAD MARX BROTHER
Groupo.

ONE OF THOSE JINGLE JANGLE MORNINGS
You may remember.

IT'S TURNED INTO TUESDAY ALWAYS TUESDAY INTO TUESDAY
And I thought today was Saturday or Sunday—though I'm ahead
    not behind.

A TAKE ON PROMISCUITY THAT NO ONE HAS OFFERED BEFORE
Look somewhere else though some things will never change.

BETTER STAY OUT OF AFRICA
That's the best way better do that nothing different.

THE TROUBLE WITH ANY RATIONAL PERSON
Sounds gestures movements colors masses.

PERSECUTED BEATEN TORTURED AND MURDERED
Rain a couple of thunderstorms a distortion of the constellations.

ZANZI [CHEMIN DE FER]
Three throws of the dice, at every throw one of the dice is left out.

THE SCROLLWORK ON THE GASKET
Obama Has Killed Osama –look at that – *Whoa –what the fuck
  just happened here?*

STAY WITH STAYING OUT THAT'S WHAT TO DO THAT'S THE POLICY
But it's just another stay-without idea from Joe Blow.

IT'S STILL FEDERAL-TRIBAL VS ANCIENT TRIBAL
Look at the natives on both sides.

DEEP AND STRONG AMONG THE RANK AND FILE
But not attendant upon the predators who have crept back onto
  the streets.

THERE SHOULD ALWAYS BE SOMEONE TO SEND
Sometimes with his choice of a partner to take care of any
  unpopular irritation.

THAT'S HOW IT USED TO BE DONE
I know but not now no more heaven forbid we should hurt
  our killer.

IT'S THE LUDIC
But much darker this time –like its original perpetrators
  centuries ago.

HEAD FAKE
But who dropped the 3 pt shot on Loping-O?

TURN IT UP [PATHOLOGY]
Better turn him her or it over first.

ABDULLAH FRÈRES
The check will reach you in Alexandria written on a London
  bank.

GRIS GRIS WARDER
Laying it down both hot and cold.

SOMETHING YOU JUST DON'T OFTEN SEE
Something else really – really something else.

SICK OF THIS SICK OF THAT
But nowhere near most or all of it.

JIN SANG FRAGILE AND DEMURE
I wish you were a pagan.

SMALL SKILLS BRIEFER IDEAS
Mediating the value of art since the mid 15th century.

SHE'S DANCING HIGH
And I can barely keep up.

THEIR IDENTIFICATION IS NOT AN EASY TASK
There's a kind of fed-up often-sullen beauty that distances them.

WOMEN WHO STAY
Stay to celebrate or stay to complain.

SOMEBODY'S TALKING TO THE RUSSIANS
It's getting darker up ahead.

EVERYTHING'S ON THE FLOOR
But nothing's off the table.

I'LL HAVE A BIGASS BROOKLYN BURGER
And I'll have a Don's Big Dago and a Rheingold.

ANTHROPOPHAGI
Tacticians of continuity.

WALDEINSAMKEIT
Another sense of isolation but not necessarily.

HE'S A GREAT IRISH MUSICIAN AND POET
But how many more times can he get beat up?

COME BACK WHAT'S GOING ON
You're doing it like a Chinese. [Chin meets Gucci]

A SMILE FROM SHIYUAN
There's pleasure in her expression she would have you know
     more fully.

CHIN AND GUCCI
Similarly nice old stuff we could start there.

AND GUCCI AND CHANEL
Who remembers exactly?

THE VARIOUS EYEWITNESSES
Departed—only not so long ago.

THE BEST USE OF THE SHOULDER
Is to peer over.

HE PUT ANOTHER DICK ON ONE
And didn't have to elaborate its use.

THERE'S ALWAYS A LOT OF CHARM IN THE WELL-HANDLED
I know her well we both *know* that's why it's so great.

I BEEN THERE BUT I NEVER TOLD NOBODY
Went far over and lost the line in Memphis.

THIS WASN'T SUPPOSED TO HAPPEN
Not anyway now like it did before.

MORE LIKE A WHISPER
I've got no reason to believe in anything now he said.

I HEAR YOU MOAN I HEAR YOU MOAN
Now I must do something but certainly nothing like what
    you'd done.

COOL BREEZES AND TRAIN WHISTLES
How rough is that?

OPENING GAMBIT [FONS ET ORIGO]
There's another Mason got another Dixon.

WELL NOT EXACTLY
Flexings of concentrated thought and expression?

I'VE GOT NO REASON TO BELIEVE IN ANYTHING NOW OR LATER
I hear you, fool, I hear you.

SOME GRISTLE IS ALWAYS NEEDED [IF ONLY TO AFFORD THE
    TEMPLATE'S SHEEN]
Found most subtly among the old masters.

AND WHO ARE YOU
What of mine is out there is still generally going around for the
    first time.

THE NEW IS ALWAYS WHAT ELUDES
Despite one's position on its necessity.

HOLLYWOOD IS BASED ON
What most easily and unsuccessfully avoids capture.

VALVES OR NO VALVES BUT A SPECIAL BULB TO DARKEN A ROOM
Can't go around now and find something that hasn't been
    measured by light.

WHEN THE ARMS ARE STRETCHED ABOVE THE HEAD
Form is lost if the structure is small.

THE RETURN OF ZINC [NYC]
You'd be sadly mistaken, señor, if you thought it ever went away.

WORKS AS HARD AS
An air conditioner in Luxor.

HOLLYWOOD SPECTACLE [SHORT DOSES]
The ongoing refinement of airbags.

HOW AMERICA SELLS IT
Staying barely level with those who sell it their own damn way.

ALL THOSE BOTTLES OF WHISKY
Finally began to fog my mind then one night.

ADDRESSING THE FORMERLY COLONIAL
You must first realize they are no longer interested in anything
    you say.

PUSHING THE SHOVEL
Is better than pulling the dirt.

THIS HAS BEEN THE TERRIBLE ABUNDANCE
Another hold on yourself.

AND NOW I'M LOOKING FOR A RIDE OUT OF TOWN
The secret's getting around.

ALL THESE WRITERS OF THE DISPARATION
Most of them anyway, and that's where the problem begins.

MOVING LEAR-AND-FALSTAFF SLOW
The failures of Iago taken as instruction.

TRUTH IS PERSONAL
Don't go to anyone for the truth.

AN ANTI-AMERICAN BOURGEOIS SELLOUT
But he might lend you some of her money.

WHAT ELSE
It can always be better.

IF HE EVER SUGGESTS SOMETHING WITH A CILANTRO WINE GLAZE
Take him outside and shoot him immediately.

CAN ALWAYS BE BLAMED ON SERIOUS HEADWINDS
What you and that young woman agreed to do.

FALSTAFF IN THE SNOW LEAR IN THE HOVEL
The joy of new and many meanings.

DIPLOMATIC BLOWBACK
Initiates an ongoing proxy war with a purported ally.

IT TOOK A DECADE
But now we're going after the rest of them full time.

BETTER THAT
Than another space station.

BUDGETARY DIETARY
Elle le décrit.

TIQUE OP
A car passing in the rain and two broken mirrors en face.

THE PROLOGUE TAKES PLACE BACKSTAGE
Spoken in a voice given a small echo.

THE REQUEST HAS JUST COME
That something be done in shaping its length.

THE REQUEST HAS COME
For determinations of the spatial secured by all that is unmediated.

A RETURN TO THE ANTIC BY WAY OF THE LUDIC
No one minds no one cares a few listen and some also smile.

NOTRESPASSING.ORG
Laser grids and guard dogs if quicksand moat is traversed or
    closed circuit video neutralized.

MAX EST FAIT PRISONNIER
Par une peuplade de femmes vampires assoiffées.

SITAH MEANS FURROW
Along which we proceed.

JESUS SAID
Just about everything.

THE BUDDHA TOO
Yes, of course, the Buddha too.

EL HOMBRE INVISIBLE CONTRA FU MANCHU
In this version almost everything takes place on earth.

STATION CHIEF
Since the raid I've been identified and am out of a job.

MIDDLE RANGE
And ever subtler phrasing.

POULENC
Lived at 5, rue de Medicis, Paris.

SEVEN RESPONSES TO TENEBRAE
Onnuvvero taviantitu mokkhu nommadima cororcyrex turru
    zemwezi.

NOT AS LATE AS EARLY
Amin hopes the Zionist paradigm will be abandoned.

NEGOTIATING PARTNERS NEVER WORKS OUT
It's a failed middle-eastern notion of a unity-front.

ZAMBEZI CENTRAL
Upriver people.

RIO DOS BONS SINAIS
Smoke and deep-river-smoothing in the crosshatch.

BY 1830
The connection had silted up.

TO THE NW IS PORT MELVILLE
Further north and beyond is Elephants Island.

CORRUPTION DEMON WORSHIP AND SORCERY
Further reasons the pump don't work.

BACK IN THE DAY
A few bottles of Dom Perignon and two Egyptian hookers.

THERE'S A GUY ON THE PHONE WHO SAYS HE WROTE A BOOK
He wants to know if you ever read it.

THE TRICK'S ONLY ALERT ENGINEER
Vaquero of the short space.

COPLAND'S APPALACHIAN SPRING OR BARBER'S MEDEA SUITE
Neither one.

JESU JOY OF SHEEP SAFELY GRAZING
Goodnight Mrs Wolfman wherever you is.

CLEAN UP AFTER PATIENCE
Required following any contact with the beloved Rachel.

ANNIVERSARIE [AFTER DONNE]
Rent's paid in full and the soul is free.

YAWK THE HAWK
Everyman one man Whitman another.

FROM SHIT TO SHINOLA
Are we moving backwards or in reverse?

BY COSMIC WATERS AND THE MIND
Always noting which came first.

FOOLUS AMERICANUS
Herr Æsel M. Holler, get yourself an eraser and a waste basket.

FIRST LOVE
A quiet garden spot near a mound of snow-covered stones.

ANCHE QUI È TUTTO A POSTO
cmyedpklajqtwrngdfsxvihuzb7426913508

THIS IS NOT A PROPER FORUM
My lawyers and Tiresias advise me.

PUT A WOLF IN THE EXTENDER
For efficiency's sake.

OTHERWISE AREAS OF FOG
Past the edge of awareness.

SECURITY EXPERT
No such thing.

VANISHING POINT
Stops vibrating in the gunsight.

DISTENDED NETWORK
Vainly persistent.

REMOVED
Then left—and rite.

ASSERTION
I'm going to change the ending and throw it in the trash.

THE TRUTH OF EMPTINESS
All nor else.

THE CULT OF NEGLECT
Gives rise to new political trends and bizarre intellectual
    groupings.

IN MOST GENTEEL COMPANY
You can prick your finger but not the reverse.

AMERIKA
No longer has allies—it only has *interests*.

SUSPECTS
Are often referred to as people of interest.

VERBATIM
The momentary effect of bad health.

THE REMAINS
In thin board covers colored red and black in a marbled pattern.

PRIMO QUADERNO DI 7047 CASA PENALE SPECIALE DI TURI
Gius. Laterza e figli, Bari [*fogli cinquanta*].

MARXISM AND FORM
We lived in a state of unparalleled self-delusion even though we
    meant well.

POLI SCI
As liturgical as every revolution –in retrospect.

PATIENCE SPEED A METHODICAL APPROACH AND INTUITION
One without all the others leads to failure.

BUCCANEERS OF VENUS
Old and new curiosa on the Vicaritron.

HERE OR THERE OR HERE OR WAY OVER THERE
But no further.

JOHN AND JANE DOUGH
Possess a highly nuanced sense of personal awareness called a
    public face.

THE ANCIENT USE OF STONE
This is not a book but an imposition –in every intended sense of
    the word.

A STUPA NOT A STELE
A personal preference is stated.

AS SIGNAL TO THE VULTURES
A fire of juniper twigs.

THE APPREHENSION OF A SMIRK
Equanimity and spite.

A FISTFUL OF BARLEY
Given from the hands of another and thrown into the wind.

UP DOWN
Neither's so different after all—especially when walking.

THE ALPHABET [ALSO QUITE COMPLEAT] BY RS
A book whose sense of form combines Paint by Number with *Plan
9 from Outer Space.*

HOT-WIRE HANGOUT
The place where one goes to get it all done. [Averroës]

HEY M'SIEU REGARDEZ-VOU
Rachel in furs with harp and drum music by Mahler.

LITTLE ORPHINK ANGLE
But no corner to be turned.

HASHISH AND HORSEPOWER
El Looneyoso Deluxe.

SMALL BALL
That's the *scope* and the *problem.*

IN SOME PRIVATE WORLD WHO ARE AÏDA AND HIME
Well, my friend, you might well ask and believe you deserve
to know.

1000 TOMBS AND 3000 ANCIENT SETTLEMENTS
Sex architecture food and physical danger, as usual.

A LITTLE MORE THAN A DECADE AFTER THE RECENT MILLENNIUM
Everyone is the enemy—everyone.

LEFTY RIGHTY SWITCH
Now you see it now you see it now you see it—damn, it's over *here.*

A SPRING DAY AT THE EDGE OF THE WORLD [LI SHANG-YIN
  812-858 A.D.]
On the edge of the world once more the day slants.

EVELYN SHIYUAN RACHEL VANESSA JIN SANG
If only for today, they—too soon *them*.

THE PRONOMINAL AS TEMPORAL
They... *them*.

A FEW MORE BRICKS IN THE POCKETS
With a sense of the contractor's need to find an immediate use.

PAROXYSMIC RADIO
Tuned seated with a little stick—a twig of wood elder is
  preferred.

A HISTORY OF THE INNER EAR
Une histoire de l'oreille interne Una storia del orecchio interno

VIRTUAL PET SHOT TO DEATH BY TROUBLED NEIGHBORHOOD BOY
Sur mes deux oreilles.

I HAVE AN APPOINTMENT WITH THE EYE DOCTOR CAN'T TALK NOW
  CAN'T TALK NOW
Carrots, m'boy, carrots—that's the only thing for it—carrots.

AN UNCOMPROMISING SENSE OF COMPONENT
Strict economy of moans.

IS THERE ANY STORY IN WHICH REVENGE IS NOT TO SOME DEGREE
  PRESENT
The unexpected coeval determination of two distinctive
  incidents relative to x.

NOT BAD
Chicago gets it right most of the time.

PROCEDURE [IN ONE STEP]
Going in going away.

SUBURB SUBORB SUBARB
Where are they now–the deceased were seen gathering fungi.

EVENTHING KEEPING PARTICULAT
And a bit of this with a wooden spoon.

A WOMAN WITH A DARK HEART
Cannot fail to be interesting.

ON THE OPENING DAY OF THE FAIR
Austen and Austin country.

WHAT YOU BECOME AWARE OF IS THE SLIGHTEST THING
I don't think that's all of it apart from piling the stones.

ON THE OTHER HAND
The ones who don't get it are still very beautiful.

OBOE CONCERTOS IN D
As long as by Vivaldi–as long as that only as long as that.

SHOWERS POSSIBLE BY MIDNIGHT A LOW OF 73
A little leftover for the dog–absolutely nothing more.

LISTEN TALK SAY
Animated by the angular.

IT'S SO OLD IT MAY BE EGYPTIAN
This is where the old begins in the immediate.

NINEFOURTHREE TWO ONE SIRENS AND HORNS
When she was with the Flying Earls.

GROWING A NICE CROP OF PEAS
Where you'd now rather grow tomatoes.

COMPLEX ANGULARITIES ANIMATED
Wondering what human flesh tastes like amid laughter.

WHAT ELSE WHAT ELSE WHAT ELSE
Opportunity, botanizing, accident, memory, rank.

MORE PEOPLE I'VE FORGOTTEN
Stephen Chaplin William Claire Robin Messing Kent
    Broadhurst John Wilson.

SANCTUARY
Always with the meaning of a place of training.

THE ABANDONED SHADOWED LENGTHS
Returned as patches of light on the wall.

STORIA DEL ORECCHIO INTERNO
Everything all of it for Satie.

THE RE AND PART AND TEE OF REPARTEE
An exploration of fou entoquiddam.

PARDON A MOMENT OF MADNESS
It's of four entoquiddam.

COLD FOOD OLD STYLE
This time you come back for the spices and with some whiskey.

UPON UPON REFLECTION
Small pieces torn with the fingers eaten and strewn selectively.

THE LONG DAY WANES
Hide or go somewhere else to work.

FACES FULL OF WHAT'S MISSING
Or what someone has taken away and put there instead.

SWEAT UNFOCUSED GLOOM AND BAD DREAMS
Consideration risk payoff.

ACOUSTICALLY GENERATED AND RESHAPED CLOUDS OF SOUND
From which only brief and tentative themes emerged.

TESTING AN HYPOTHESIS AGAINST OBSERVABLE FACTS
I love you can you see that are you aware of that?

LOVING
How about if I do this did you see that can you see what it
     means?

PACK MY BAG
Shoot, a fella could have a pretty good time in Dallas with all this
     stuff.

NOTHING
Pronounced [as did the Elizabethans] noting.

THE EAVESDROP
As in *much ado about.*

HEAD QUARTERS
Red Turkish carpets and hand-painted murals.

A LONG HISTORY OF SECRETS AND DESIRES
Symmetrical knotting.

CHANCE OR DESIGN OR CHANCE DESIGN
Like softly expanded red and gold pagodas.

SMALL FEET
Never trust anyone with small feet.

THIN LIPS
A sure sign of cruelty.

PITEOUS ADMISSIONS
The violins are far too busy and the cellos of course can't keep
    up.

A CONFLUENCE OF FACTORS
Stephanie of memory and Shurong of the present day.

MR AND MRS EXPENSIVE SHOES
Sorrowful sharp faced sturdy and strong—like their brogans.

GOODBYE MR WONG
Big badge big belt no gun.

WHERE I WAS TOLD I NOW LIVE
In a small room with a table a chair and a microphone
    connected to a loudspeaker.

BE HERE EVEN WHEN YOU'RE ANYWHERE ELSE BE HERE
You've been counted.

WHERE I BELIEVE I NOW LIVE
In a gray stone building next to the pithead winding gear.

WITHOUT THOUGHT OF FAME OR PROFIT
Just gimme my pay and shut up about it.

AH YES LOGICK
He's a blue collar guy but he wants to be successful.

WOULD YOU MIND IF I
You don't appear to be doing anything else with your body right
    now.

AN INTIMACY
Here's where I help you lose your blues.

THE BOOK IS DONE
Send a mule or a helicopter but come and get me.

A NEW PLANET
Of course, fool, no one lives there.

A RUIN WITH A VIEW
Why I came here.

PERMANENT
Permanent, yes—but far from thorough.

MOST OF THEM FEATURING SHEEP
19th c. rustic paintings and recent poetry anthologies.

HOW TO WRITE
Conjoin preformed elements and adjust their intricate
    boundaries.

ACCIDENTAL INCIDENTAL OR SENTIMENTAL
None of the above—now what?

MEMORIES OF FRESH AIR THE SUN UPLAND MEADOWS AND
    OVERHANGING TREES
Et in Arcadia ergo [sic/seek/push in].

EFFECTIVE MINIATURIZATION
It's very expensive, very expensive, very.

A LITTLE LEFTOVER FOR THE DOG
The same from the same to the same.

YOU GOT TO READ IT CAREFUL
Because I'm talking right to you.

PITEOUS ADMISSIONS II
He awoke the next morning and turned his face to the
    window – no the wall.

REPETITION IS NOT SO MUCH THE MOTHER OF INVENTION
But invariably leads to the discovery of further often unexpected
    subtle discernments.

ABSTRACTING THE FINGERS
Abstracting the figures.

FORMS OF COMPLETENESS
Questioned in the midst of expression.

WRITING SLOWLY ENOUGH
For the ink to flow through the letters.

FORMALHAUT
Negotiator of the viatic but ever low on the horizon.

MUCH AS THE MIDDAY
He speaks upward.

ATTENTION WRITTEN
Words of the knotted edge.

NUMB FOOT ON THE MARBLE STEPS
Where the I emerges.

THE SPINE OF THE COLOSSUS
A decaying wick.
TURNING THROUGH THE DISTINCTIONS
In search of a logical sequence.

HOW IT'S DONE
Of by of.

THE PARENTHETIC
The wager of the wedge that opens from the with out.

KEEP UP NOW BECAUSE I'M ALREADY GONE
Running down the road trying to loosen my load.

HEY FOOL
I got your jingle-jangle morning—I got your jingle-jangle *right
here.*

BEAUTIFUL DANCERS GOURMET MEALS
And the opportunity to contract some exotic diseases.

YOU CAN ASK AND YOU CAN ASK AND YOU CAN ASK
But I'm not going to say.

DER ZAUBERBERG
I'm looking at your heart he said in a suppressed voice.

CORONAL EJECTION
Followed by an auroral alert.

IN CASE OF AN EMERGENCY BREAK GLASS
But be sure you finish what's in it first.

ANOTHER WAY OF GETTING IT DONE IN THE SHORT TERM
E lascia pur grattar dov'è la rogna!

NOSTRUM
To stop sneezing or hiccups place your lips gently to the nostrils
of a she-mule.

ALL ERRORS IN FACT
Should be attributed to the intentional *charta incondita* nature
of this work's composition.

QUOTH THE RAVEN *EVERFOR*
The rules are a little crazy but then I'm not from around here.

JUST DON'T
Don't throw a shoe–in any sense of the action.

BUILT ON ESTRANGEMENTS AND DISLOCATIONS
The contiguous and continuous partly *taken* partly *supplied.*

DYING HALF WAY
Half dead or not making it any further beyond midpoint.

PARTICIPATORY NEUTRALITY
A plank a small sharp stick paper a pot of India ink and 100
    acres of surrounding veldt.

REPUTATION THEN REPEAT
A commemorative and complimentary resolution with a
    parasitic capacity.

COMPLETING THE SUSPENSION
Things to number and question turn over don't ignite.

SLOWER STARTS IN SUMMER
With colossal effort and little attention amazed to be starting out
    so far ahead.

IT ASHES OVER IN THE FADING SUNLIGHT
Memories you may have wished to apply to the initiative.

ZEPPELINO ZEPPELINI THE REMOVER OF HEIGHTS
The rain extends all the way up the coast with snow in the
    higher elevations.

STACCATO FORMOSO OF THE OVERHEAD FAN
A wilderness of symmetries put between the genial forager and
    the bumping shadow.

SCATTERED FOOTPRINTS NEAR THE GATE
Premonitions of folly that occasioned the need for a structure
    such as this.

EVENTOGRAPHY
Headlong and learnedly coarse–the rhythm lets you pick up
    what you need.

GIZMO REPLACEMENT COMES INTO ITS OWN
Premonitions of folly that occasioned the need for a device like
    this.

NO ALLEGIANCE NO CHARM
Never quite hearing what you think you said–every idea and
    every other idea.

WHAT'S SEEN UNIQUELY PRESENT
Afford the best grain along which to cut.

HE REGARDS THE BOOKS HE WRITES
As a service to those who have misplaced his address.

A WHEEL PATCHED WITH A SHOE
The answer is more mysterious than predictive.

EVERY SCORE MUST BE SETTLED
Every note played.

CHORD CHANGES ARE ALWAYS VERY PERSONAL
He continues to organize accidents and call them
    appurtenances.

A LIFE-SIZED DICTION
After all our subtle color and nervous rhythm.

NEITHER INSENSIBLE NOR OF ANCIENT ACCENT
Not so much indolent as casually migratory.

NOTARY SOJAC
Shame's collectivist propensities are unavoidable.

AMONG THE NOBLE LAMBERTINI OF BOLOGNA [1746]
Wearing an ermine-lined cape [*mozzetta*] and hat [*camauro*]
    characteristic of winter garb.

MUHAMMAD ZAMAN
Creator of a well-known series of 17th century Persian iris
    studies soon often imitated.

RIGHT BRAIN LEFT BRAIN
Write brain wrong brain.

URDU AND FARSEE AND YIDDISH
Try hearing the singer *and* the song.

THE I'S HAVE IT AND EYES DON'T
Everything is a process—even that which isn't.

CONTINUOUS SEARCH
Improvisation not Fibonacci.

LIFE IS REVENGE
See if you qualify.

MORE HONKY LOGICK
If there's a major drought, fool, how're people going to pee—go
    ahead answer me that.

IT'S IMPORTANT THAT I KNOW
So give me your own flawed version.

SHRED OF DECENCY
It's *always* in shreds.

PARADIGM SHIFT
The barely perfected nature of a paradigm is one of
    shape-shifting.

ACCORDING TO PASOLINI [AND OF COURSE I AGREE]
Tira più un pelo di fica che un carro di buoi.

A PASSEGGIATA DELLA VERGOGNA
The worse time to be objective is when there is no objective.

ST FRANÇOIS PARLANT AUX OISEAUX
One side of the conversation is still a matter of earnest
    speculation.

SOMETHING COLD IN A BOWL
Served in failed compensation with words of dispirited counsel.

BURLESQUE BY NATURE
No other way—even in Nature.

IN THE FADING LIGHT
Parrots *hoik*, donkeys bray, dogs howl, bright winds defray the
    penumbra.

THE PULL TO PRONOUNCE AND THE YANK OF THE HE[A]RD
The unexpected the unanticipated made ready.

HOLE LEVEL
Not *this* here but that *there*.

TOO SLOW TO MEASURE TOO QUICK TO LOCATE
That which the geometric occludes and its derivatives prevent.

THE SUM OF OLD AND NEW WORDS
Uncertainties and peculiarities advancing on the closing page.

WARHORSE WAREHOUSE
A place we'd all wish to avoid.

THE TOWN OF VITRIOL
I seriously doubt you'll find it in Canada or in any of the
    Scandinavian countries.

THE FUTURE OF CORPORATE OWNERSHIP
Their milk, cheese, and butter are the best—but only in a moral
    sense.

A BOMB WAS PLACED IN THE SPACIOUS APARTMENT ACROSS FROM
    THE ELEVATORS
But first the young wife was murdered upon answering the
    door.

DRUNKEN BIRDS AT CHIN-HEIGHT
Privilege the moments complex to the limits of resource.

VICO'S PRE-ORDAINED CYCLICISM
Animated measures of distance—not fragments—simply never
    the same route twice.

PAZZIA AND ITS UNCOMMON DENOMINATORS [SELF-SUSPICION AND
    SKEPTICISM]
It reaches it does not extend nor does it re-solve.

INTO THE GROOVE OF THE VANISHING LINE
From place to place suits every action.

AT THE MOST BASIC MECHANISTIC LEVEL
How eclipses why and what.

ALCHEMY WITH AN AUDIENCE
The *performance* of solution—the first recourse.

FRAGILE SYMMETRIES GOVERN THESE APPROXIMATIONS
Nucleate, the orbits resume their circuits prolonging inanition
after a single circuit.

WE DON'T GET IT THEY SAID
What are you waiting for—it to get you?

TUNELESS AND EQUIDISTANT
Genuine, commonplace, flawed, in perfect proportion.

A RARE SITING
A blonde over there in the smoke gazing into a compact and
smiling.

TELEPHONOSCOPE TELEPHONOGRAPHIC TELEPHONOSCOPOGRAPHIC
*Consider what all these devices have done—can I now hook you up
with one of the finest?*

WEAPON SONGS
Best performed in the attitude of an exasperated head waiter
taking an order.

SEED CAFÉ SAID CAFÉ SAD CAFÉ
Are you staying—or have you just been left behind?

HOW HAVE YOU CONDUCTED YOURSELF IN THIS LIFE
Because now awaiting you on the other side are 72 vegans.

COLONY COLLAPSE DISORDER
A new restaurant must now be found for these our regular
meetings.

MONSANTO NOW OWNS ALL THE SEEDS
This can't be good—can't be good for nature—can't be good for
anyone.

INDUSTRIALIZED QUEEN BREEDING WEAKENS GENETIC STOCK
This is in reference to *Apis mellifera* and not whatever else you
might be thinking.

THEIRE
An accidental configuration, yes—but quite appropriate when
closely considered.

I AM OWED 15 POINT 5 MILLION DOLLARS
You know where I'm going with this don't you—how about
yourself?

PERCEIVED COLLABORATORS [SUCH AS YOURSELVES]
Weren't—but as always the perception was useful politically.

BUT ONLY IF AND WHEN I'M ASKED
Irish whisky, Asian women, Turkish tobacco, and American
music.

MORAL BALANCE
*An awareness of the banal—suddenly or conditioned in the long
term—is the best reality check.*

FROM A RELIABLE SOURCE
I heard about a tree that's 5000 years old. There's not much that
tree doesn't know.

SMIRKING OEDIPAL CRANK
Biased, corrupt, and linked to the cia.

THE ACRES NEEDED TO SUPPORT ONE COW
Do not come to everyone.

YESTERDAY TODAY AND TOMORROW
We still have one day left to talk, but it's only one day.

QUIET STARS AND QUIET CHORDS FROM MY GUITAR
And something that rhymes with afar, or jar, or car, or tar, or
   Lamar, or cigar.

HOW THEY DID IT
Navis ex arboris trunco igne excavata.

PROPORTIONAL HARMONIES OF VOLUMES AND VOIDS
Plus ça change, plus c'est la même chose.

NIGHT IS THE SHADOW OF THE EARTH [HOMAGE TO PARMENIDES]
The moon keeps looking at the sun. When it blinks it causes
   the tides.

TEMPLES AND TENEMENTS [A PATTERN LANGUAGE]
Where's the kitchen where's the bedroom where's the bathroom
   where's the altar?

IT WAS ALL VERY WARM AND ALL VERY INTERESTING
But I would have preferred to see dance get off its knees and
   back on its feet again.

THE WALKING THE HUNGER THE COLD THE KIDNAPPING
It's like I'm coming back for the 6th time.

IN THE SHADOW OF THE GUARD TOWER BETWEEN THE COOKHOUSE
   AND THE SHED
Once we're beyond the barbed wire stay low and make a run for
   the woods.

REGARDING THE WRITERS OF BLURBS AS A GROUP [OR, YOU NEVER
   KNOW]
*I think these motherfuckers do it only because they must all share a
   very rare blood type.*

DON'T MAKE PO' RAYMOND GET OUT THIS CAR WITH HIS GUN NOW
You better hurry up and stop that texting while you're driving.

CULTURE MOOD FASHION AND ARCHITECTURE
If you're advancing the frontier, occasional failure should be
expected.

MAD SQ
Being out of the show was more important to me than being in
the show.

THE THEATRICALITY OF THE EMPTY SPACE [OR, *FURTHER
ABRIDGING THE ENSEMBLE*]
The best action is when the ceiling collapses and the walls fall
in. It's highly emotional.

SILENT ETHOS WHEN IT'S THERE
Isn't it always? Though I could be in error.

IN WHICH DIRECTION ARE YOU HEADED NORTH EAST OR SOUTH
Oui oc si—or all directions at once? The enduring mongrel
barks in every rival idiom.

I GOT HER BACK IN MY ARMS AGAIN
And Flo, she don't know, 'cause the man she loves is a Romeo.

FROM THE GLOSSARY
Values—See Criteria.

CRITERIA
Whatever the hell is important to you.

THE VALUE ABOVE A VALUE
How much can your wallet hold?

FRONTMAN
There's absolutely no point in being any other kind.

DON'T BOTHER LOOKING HERE
For what Dante called *la gentilezza*—it's been intentionally
removed. Worn away.

CIRCA 1295 BY STRETCHING A POINT
Philosophers and so-called men of letters could become members of the Guild of Apothecaries.

WHAT ELSE MIGHT BE CONSIDERED AND SOLD AS A DRUG
Let's climb up higher on this mountain and see all that's to be found on the next terrace.

THE NECESSARY PIVOT
Wobbling or unwobbling, swerving or unswerving, accomplishing the pivot is always necessary.

CHARGED WITH ONE COUNT OF STILL LOOKING GUILTY
□件人： □送□□： 主□： 原始□件：

KEYNESIAN REDISTRIBUTION
We owe money to China and they don't want our opium anymore—or not quite as much.

ONCE YOU TAKE AWAY THE NORMAL RESPONSES TO PAIN COMES CRUDE MANIPULTION
But that's just plain old politics.

HOW TO GET SOMEWHERE IN A HURRY AND LOOK GOOD WHILE DOING SO
Hire an 800-pound gorilla, and avoid at all times being one yourself.

THE GLITTERING DEPOSIT
Sprinkled with gold and diamond dust, it's still shit—because shit will always be shit.

HANS VAN MEEGEREN AND PIERRE BRASSAU
Or your name here.

EXAGGERATED FOR EMPHASIS
1+1

HOMAGE TO SPICER

On July 8, 1953 Robin Roberts' streak of 28 consecutive complete games pitched ended.

ONLY YOU KNOW HOW FULL OF SHIT YOU ARE

However, I believe we can add this one to the list of usual suspects as well.

RCBS

Fractious spooks in the brokedown machine.

AFTER CATULLUS

Twenty-five in one night seems at the moment to be the number to beat.

EN ROUTE

From whose to hers from whose to his.

SENECA MAINTAINED

The world was a better place before there were architects.

H$_2$O

He also pointed out there couldn't be anyone else out there because there was too much water.

NEGOTIATING A DYNAMIC ENVIRONMENT AND TESTING THE LIMITS OF HIERARCHY

Welcome to the jungle, welcome to the desert, welcome to the mountains, welcome to the streets.

TRAPPED IN NOT BY AMBIVALENCE

Few voices and many naked bodies.

I WAS DISGUISED AS A VASE OF RED TULIPS A VAQUERO OF THE FLOODED DIKES

Getting better never stuck in neutral.

EXAGGERATED FOR EMPHASIS II
999,999,999,999,999,999,999,999,999,999,999,999,
999,999,999,999,999,999,999,999,999,999,999,99999

THIS CANNOT BE MADE PLAINER
I want the product, *not its special name, or any therefore related to
its chemical breakdown.*

THE CREDIBILITY OF THE OFFERING
Is still under consideration by the rank and file and their better-
dressed shop stewards.

UNLESS IT DISPLEASES THE SUNNE
Well-informed and willing to take risks, my shadow pursues
you.

BORN DURING CONSULIBUS AULO HIRTIO ET GAIO VIBIO PANSA
AUC 711
Digitized in shades of green and blue, surfaces flattened into
edge.

DON CICCIO GLARED AT THE MSGR WHOSE NAME WAS DON NICOLA
He paid on time like everybody else *–or else.*

FAMA VOLAT
How was he to know? he shouted in explanation –about to turn
mean.

A RECORD OF HAPPENINGS AND OCCASIONS FROM INSIDE THE
OUTSIDE WORLD
During and according to breaks in the action and amid the
awareness of their rhythms.

BUSINESS LUNCH IN PITTSBURGH OR OMAHA
Everyone's on time and almost everyone's relaxed.

ROUTINE
When you play 162, routine is very important.

WHEREVER YOU BAT IN THE LINEUP [FINE PRINT]
*You will always be expected to hit in the clutch whether someone's
on base or not—remember that.*

JETER GETS HIS 3000TH GOES 5 FOR 5 STEALS A BASE AND KNOCKS
IN THE WINNING RUN
This is the way we expect it should always be played because it's
baseball.

HIT WITH POWER AND PULL THE BALL
Put it where they aren't like in every other sport.

PRUDENCE AND JUSTICE ARE A HARD MIX
Seeking opportunities to travel to and cover difficult locations,
fluent in 5 languages.

FOR Z IS THE GREATER PART OF GENOESE SPEECH
And this letter cannot be enunciated without great harshness.

LET'S HURRY UP AND EAT
We don't have [*Manchiamo introque*] anything better to do [*che
noi non facciamo altro.*]

IT ALL BECOMES CLEAR WHEN YOU SIT DOWN AND THINK ABOUT IT
And it's quite a process: sit down, think, whereupon: the soon
arrival of clarity.

ALL HAT AND NO RANCH
In the philosophical sense: he's dealing with one and coming to
terms with the other.

DARK SIDE OF THE MOON [FOR EP]
It was hope more than pleasure—but now with you here it's
pleasure more than hope.

UN ORECCHIO ASSOLUTO
With this in my possession everything I say must be believed
  and trusted.

AMONG BRIMMING RIVERS AND DEEP CLEAR MERES WHERE SHAFTS
  OF SUNLIGHT PIERCE
*The dense foliage of the trees and lay with the shifting shadows on
  the grass.* "Hello...Who?"

SOMEBODY GET UP AND SING
How about the lovely young woman over there?

HAVE YOU SEEN MY GOLF BAG
No, but I found your needle.

AND NOW A MESSAGE FROM HECTOR OF HARLEM
The sources of the dark earth, misty Hell, the undraining sea,
  all, all dank and dismal.

NO ONE WANTED TO TAKE THAT RIDE
They're looking for someone to figure it out.

IF IT'S SOMETHING YOU NEED
Then it's something I'm better off without.

I HAVEN'T SEEN YOU BEFORE
Then by all means enjoy the view.

IF YOU BUILD IT THEY WILL COME
*We did and it's been a while, so if they don't get here soon we're
  going to pack it all up and leave.*

CAIN AND NIMROD
A couple very early city planners—Cain died in the collapse of
  one of his own buildings.

DEMONYM
*A gentilic, the name for a person of a particular locality—their books
and stones can be read.*

I'M NOT MAKING THREATS I'M STATING RIGHTS
The attitude of the outside world is therefore not of interest
to me.

WITH SADNESS BY ONE AND WITH JOY BY ANOTHER
A purposeful restraint is simultaneously realized and fully
accepted by both.

THE VESSEL FIRST LISTED TO THE STARBOARD AND THEN SANK IN
GOOD WEATHER
Big, clean stories of outdoor life.

DOOMED TO DIE AS VICTIMS OF DESERT JUSTICE
Men disguised as angry bears attack a group of men disguised
as rampaging bulls.

HOW CAN SLIM CHANCE AND FAT CHANCE MEAN THE SAME THING
You must have some idea and I'd be one who's interested in
hearing it.

SOUTH AND TO THE EAST AND WEST
Death and dying among those whose ability to trick and deceive
helped them survive.

THE STREETS OF DAMASCUS
Not now, Raimundo—says Toufik Rajah Ibrahim—no, I mean 50
years ago.

MUZZLE FLASH
August light on pitted chrome.

AIN'T THAT PRETTY AT ALL NEVER WAS NEVER WILL BE CAN'T BE
No pretty there ever—of all the pretty there ever's been.

OWNING THE SPACE OF YOUR VOICE
Allows for the construction of the interpreter's house.

THE THEATRICAL AS MEANS TO AN END
Does very little to advance what else is going on in the room.

A HARD GREEN RAY JUST ABOVE AND ALONG THE HORIZON'S
    EVENING RED
The constituent harmonies of expectation and sighting per
    occasion per occasion.

PINE FOR BURNING AND LAUREL FOR INCENSE
For by beans was the Magistrate elected in some parts of
    Greece.

A CAUTION IS ONLY IMPLIED BY THE RELUCTANT HERO'S ARRIVAL
    FROM AN UNKNOWN
Or distant place he was forced to leave when accused of a crime
    he didn't commit.

UNKNOWN OR DISTANT
How far is far or *far enough*–here–or here–how about here–or
    over here–or *here*?

TESTICULIS MISERI DEXTRAS SUBDUCITE
Like most else, more easily said, more easily advised, than done.

THE GREATEST DISTANCE BETWEEN TWO POINTS
Means to be ever on the move.

STRUCK IN THE EYES BY THE SMOKE OF SACRIFICE
Makes it almost impossible to judge by appearances alone.

WHAT LIES NEAREST AT HAND
Should always be rejected–think of the choices made by
    Melville's orchard robbers.

MASSIVE ETHICAL LAPSES
*Mouthing talking points, conspiracies, bombing embassies,
    assassinations, warlords, and poppies.*

THE WALKING THE HUNGER THE COLD THE KIDNAPPING
It's like I'm coming back for the 6th time.

IN THE SHADOW OF THE GUARD TOWER BETWEEN THE COOKHOUSE
    AND THE SHED
Once we're past the barbed wire make a run for the woods.

TEMPLES AND TENEMENTS [A PATTERN LANGUAGE]
Where's the kitchen where's the bedroom where's the bathroom
    where's the altar?

WE'RE NOT INTERESTED IN CONSTRUCTIVE CRITICISM OR
    EGO-ABUSE ON EITHER SIDE
We just want a raise in pay.

ANY FIRST FUCK
Always the deal breaker–no going back afterwards.

CASA PENALE SPECIALE DI TURI 8 FEBRUARY 1929
Impronte simultanee delle quattro dita lunghe della mano
    destra.

THE BOAT ROCKS
Aching fathoms gather the tides and ghosts into particular times
    of day.

IMPLEMENTS OF BIAS
Axe handles, beer, bullhorns, badges, and dogs.

BREITENFELD 1631 SMALL FIELD ARTILLERY MANEUVERED BY HAND
    ADDED WEIGHT
To volleyed small arms fire–their shock effect followed by pike
    and cavalry charges.

THE GREATER DEAD
It's best not to mess around with their kind of fun—but I
    always do.

AND THE SUPREME POWER OF LOVE
No one's above saying so.

UNLIKE THE LIMINAL
A border by definition is what draws people to it.

LEVAI LI OCCHI [JUST A REMINDER]
La vostra donna, ch'è morta, obliare.

SHOW SOME COURAGE IT'S TIME NOW
To get those words out of your heart and into your mouth so
    everyone can hear them.

Manhattan, Paris, Bordeaux,
and Hudson, NY, 1991-2011

SALT PLUMES

A pleat of light has been here twice
back to the day and the day back
a bearing refused at its source
the stalled mercury fused in its glare
with no conjecture to mark the limit
the motion is modified

convolutions of ancient scripts
half drawn half animal birth

the arch of the back

one surface
one depth
one changing shape

an apology for
crossing the pulse of offspring

•

Uncommon offerings commonly intuited
a wooden bowl with a gilded edge
five dark stone knives
a small clasped vessel for oil with a floating wick
flanked by two wax birds

space is a factor whose
mapping disturbs
our conversation
a prospect of careful planes
tended by argument and birdsong
then abandoned to palindrome

the flex of barrier
and immaculate reticence
relent in equal shares unseparated

by edge or rhythm's orientation

amid the subtle claims of threnody
no other sense of praise
than wonder

•

Predation
mythic proxy inflected
the unanimous struggle of particulars
primed in situ
white for decay
red for the eye
blue beneath the snow

a cold wind noticed too late
now equitably disposed
something brought to completion
though the worm was in it
beyond the forms of Baal

•

Emptied markers burning in the ruts

deliberative motives
more in balance than real
fixtures of an arguing anxiety
more generous less fragile

neglected by speculation
plainest increase finds the barb
in the morose distortions of small forms
and the thin yellow words of the infatuation

it brings its own set of questions

like something brought to be abandoned
by the side of the road

•

Description is what has been taken away
the infinite lost in the simulacrum of displacement

a number not in arrangement but farther on
not in the distance but insistence

the hours gained in anonymity
the years lost word by word

contradicted by the myopia of its internal logic
uphill favors sediment

imago the gift imparted
the cross-eyed shuffle of expedience

too late the song too late the door flies open
too late the spoken mercies too late the fabric bone

•

Wandering ligatures accelerate expansion
to primary acquisition

nomadic recourse
absorbed in gerundive detail
reclaims the discretionary pursuit

essentials
the exactions of light
extolling the riot of genetic ambivalence

no ulterior duplicates
no·delivered verges
in shallow equilibrium

only the instruments make rapid movements
adapting to internalized mechanisms
adjusted by accretion

•

Proliferation
and impossible replicas

regret or loss
become a gesture for that limit

schemes of evidence
offered in contradiction

•

As intimate as doubt
all that is personal in chance
distinguishes one to one from
the one from the other

reinterpreted in the dark
and shared only with number
the objects in the room
the articles on the desk

are an assent to a consequent perfection
that is abandoned in moving on
pursuing neither a conclusion nor
a new point of entry

what had become unacceptable
is now overburdened only partially remembered
timed to the word denied with nothing
else to take its place or make its order

sustained by mechanism and the simulation
of some capable version or familiar resource
a preemptive predecessor quietly virtual provides
something other than an option

July-August, 2001

AGORA

1
Never solved the world within
the world without
come from so far
set in the right place proposing
morning already securing
not harmony but something put to the test
neat footprints in the snow
that have fallen through eleven floors
accountable to the dream
and its unfinished storm
radiant and exacting
lit by a solemn burning of wood
crouchings gala and interpreters ancient
scavenge a torpid enlightenment

2
lights before and after the flood
the slowly brightening face an
oddity of conviction
an alchemy of cadence
a bundle of printed documents
tied together with broad red tape
alias upon alias
misattributions of mood or belated prophecy
brittle and occulted by
a deposition of mirrors
deeper and deeper in the overlook
the rose-ace snagged
in a loop of ash lifted by
the mordant scuff of plumes
a parody of piety and shame
the arcane restraints of restitution

3
inexact as step from step
the desert the clarity beyond

any sense of memorized time
extruded from the lurk of symbol
prelude is stray measure
lengthening the complexions of sleep
its perfected vexations are
attrition and query in
a cartouche of ropes and weeds
pictograms and night signals
arrangements of names
fill a folklore of fragments
the sample of one and its reflection
canonic sentiments and
makeshift paradoxes
a panel of yellow light
on a faded ochre wall

4
surprises fed on disappointed warnings
extended by the blowing sands
to any creature hanging on the guess
fever or birdsong passed through degrees
and textures of preliminary sound
first before first before first
interdiction as a mode of chagrin
the moon unraveling
drifts across her eyes assessing a river life
eyes that look back
infinity summoned by color

5
Four circular rooms
of varying sizes contiguous
to a central rectangular room
There are no windows
or compromise with light
The chalk lines of the builder
after three hundred years

still mark the limits of the central room
a reciprocation of the codices
of Euclid and the dimensions
abstracted from the quarry
The eye goaded by conceit
is pulled away from every corner
to the arcs beyond
The absence of features
indicates disquiet and
a regard for wholeness
and decided mass
held within the centrifugal
sweep of the cloister

6
sound falls on your name
this is what the hands have done
to make their preference known
a word at a time
a miracle of hanging air
the remainder a phenomenon of foreground
the luminous air's
separation from all migrating birds
under whose scrupulous motion
you stand reading a letter
contrived of veiled concessions
and the moving parts of an apology
an ill-assorted collection
of hagglers in bird masks

7
a snap of flint
more syntactic than lexical
no longer a part of the city
always six hours behind the sun
certain ideas and symbols keep occurring
excuses for newsprint facts

of a short-lived dream
held in hand to
fade away more quickly
its emphatic secrecy
dado and scrollwork
lit from behind

8
recast is the discard
episode and admonition
the metaphysics that interferes
the patinas of an internal life
what turns from the center
reenacting the doubt
with grinding intuition
an owl vamping
its sense of the dark
the run of the sky
of sound of words
spoken on a road
that ebbs away

9
handwritten letter shapes
fill the page
animation dismantles anarchy
the testimony left
a mobius a zero dilated upon a zero
what is exemplary is unnamed
every day's jagged edges
broken under the tongue
a ratio moving from fact to facet
directs the sound by light
surviving the r's and l's m's and n's
maps and pawns

10
invented to be described
sent instead of given
nothing of it remains
what else is there
what is in the breakers
what deduction
what do they count to each other
facing one facing
I could hear the words
but other words separated me
from what they meant
to pronounce or recall
the buffalo and the white whale
their epic qualities seen in new places
amid a failed sense of duty

11
a famous subtraction
preserved in red lacquer
only bread and hypnotism
permit its proper name
a yellow sky set against
a grey circle of moving clouds
the closer to the sun
the more important
a given surface
nothing moves
following the circle

12
a brutal flatness
a kind of modesty
no water only ink
drained from the inner ear
a few sentences scratched
in the dirt with a match

cold as smoke
analogs and conclusions drawn
from certain isolated facts
six plus five minus nine plus
seven minus three plus six
a circle ever thinner
five plus three minus five
plus seven minus one
hand and eye turning
one upon one

13
the final version
left on the tongue
what has been said
change and depiction
placed side by side
as second thought
drops of the flood traces
of the adduced revelation
a scrimped oblivion
of imagined privileged moments
anxious with surmise

14
agreement is subversion
of direct action
what matters cannot
be remembered or named
shelves of books tilted paintings
and scattered papers
the damp-stained walls
a lament that achieved
some general expression
just another set of terms
confided to its own alphabet
every mark of punctuation

isolated and repeated two
or three times along
the bottom of every page
elements in the embodiment
of second-hand privacies

15
printed in red ink
and 100 point type on folio
sheets of grey paper
all the street-smart words
not who but when
not where but why
determine their accuracy
a translation indebted
to an associative procedure
involving interpolations of motive
corresponding to mutually
identified expressions of debt
once familiar and dependent
now confined and continuous
nothing given nothing shared
nothing taken nothing lost

16
speaking for one whose name
was never recalled who spoke
for one whose name was never known
no more than a guess
an assembled story of themselves
scenes in a hymn sung
in total darkness
the page left unfinished
bearing no dates as
is the custom when scarce
and isolated things are rendered
at the limits of a coherent life

run along a pavement radius
over the lip of an horizon
that barely spans a desk
a wall and a ceiling

17
in the jungle thirty miles
from the capitol
patience wears thin
there was no such man
kept in a room
blindfolded and poorly fed
a number with a story
about another number
an emerald dealer stands
under an elm whose branches
touch the ground he
has nowhere else to look
what time is it he asks
are you leaving right now
it's been the twelfth of the month
for at least a year
nothing else pulled from another pocket
improper distances improper time
obedient to but unmoved by the sun

18
dust lifted from a reference
intuition error and stubborn conviction
it still may happen
an unnamable point of view a prediction
closer to a legal right than a need to be said
given a colloquial emphasis
suspicion slowed to a start
the wrong person in the right place
at the wrong time
the next direction anything off the map

exposure pushed between the dark drifts
against the far wall

19
black red white and grey knots
in thick threads of similar hue
a tally of tributaries and moments
of silence put to use while old doubts
persist as a species of luck
more what the bones say when the water
floats them than the fable that explains
how the practice of waterbones began
all that's certain is that there was some
point to placing the windmill in a valley
rather than on any of the adjoining hills
but something about the feigned civility
that tempered the lengthy explanation
made the windmill and the shadow it cast
as suspect as the thistle offered for a handshake

20
100 miles of road say it's okay to want something
after all something broken will always
conspire with anything impartial
first person to first person
glare provides for any lack of detail
overhead the seasons get easier
the scarecrow totems of the uninitiated
as uncomplicated as they are cautionary
the only thing to do when they blow over
if they turn up head or feet first
is to step around but never over them

1998-2001

OBEDIENT LAUGHTER

"A goose was fattened to death . . .
and the pig will no doubt
be butchered at any moment."
                        −Kafka

Because of the person you are and the arrangement in which
you now find yourself to have agreed, all of this spread before
you has been given to you in such abundance for no other
reason. But you mustn't think of this as a way clear. There is
much here, but it won't last forever. Though you do appear judi-
cious in all things up to now. That's probably why you're still
here among us. Ingrained, no right now about it when it comes
to that. A mongrel clear of the rabid. You've even managed to
fatten-up a little, which is admirable. To mutual good purpose
at heart. Later all this will seem a paltry sum. The stretch from
punctuation to punctuation to chapter to chapter. All the mixed,
doubled, and abbreviated, advanced in splendor and squalor by
seriation. Linear ceremonies full of complex movements, abun-
dant qualifications slowly developing into the thematic. Have,
here take what I've had and fashioned into something else for
you. This will explain everything, full of where and when plus
an eye and a word or two for that, with a unique sense of testi-
mony, once again is all.

At the angles and on the flanks are found
the bravest and those most skilful with their weapons.
This configuration is for profitable maintenance
to obtain with maximum efficiency and dispatch

a specific other outcome. Fragments of the ulterior
are always left behind. One of the collective dispositions
of history. Letting some other distant time and place
to some other time and place. Trade goods, books,

paintings all tossed over the edge. One upon the other
ending beside the other. And now come briefly to rest.
All that once filled a room. Raw wood well carpentered
is what you get. Fir in some places, the doors for instance,

and not pine. Cedar panels built into the closets 150 years ago.
Continuous behavior, the convected turns and twists inscribed,
gathered, and centralized. Song turning into talk. Drums,
tambourines, recorders, oboes, and flutes. Half held, half a
    tangle.

Who first took it and named it thus? Buried its first guise
    forever.
Turned it over and out, added to it and took away, losing
and then adding a reference point. More light, any light, less
safety, a struggle to navigate, headlong into the parchment.

Speaking aloud, naming places
even those that no longer or ever existed
there is a world above for the world below.

Canopied doorways diplomacy stalled and
in the near distance a horse crossing a blue meadow
with a charming wooded hill in the background.

A hope that the north takes back the south and elsewhere
among others that the south takes back the north and still
further elsewhere the north and south become one.

What else in alleviation would you bring close?
The bait always looks desperate.
Take some of it. Think of it as food. Go elsewhere with it.

Where else would you go? What else would you find there?
   [*Where resembles*
Who put it there? Is it your real reason for coming? [*what in*
Apologies offered for any moments of good fortune. [*which*
   ways?]

He hit a fallen tree. Other matters of containment were still
   primary.
Presumed slid under the door. You couldn't miss it.
Making your own good terms on the far side of the central
   skeleton.

Write the other.

The wise man warns him
availing the same firebrand
with which the madman burneth the tent.
Charmed stones from the modern pharmacopoeia,
Protracted elevations among other actions
And bodily deportment guided by rubrics –
Running dying maimed cut crushed beaten robbed
Strangled raped murdered –hungry sick bored
Desperate lonely remorseful angry cruel feverish
Crippled empty bewildered sobbing fearful –

Brevatim et seriatim
and hunter gatherer science.

All this could be revisited later
When they change their way of thinking.
It's bound to happen. Marking time,
Certain occurrences, certain encounters,
Who prevails, who doesn't, what else
As a result has entered the picture.
Thumbing through it . . .
The time is right. The place is right.
What else is missing?
A strong central flame from a single candle –
The future will find other ways. It has up to now.
Then all of this can be realized quite
Differently, held up, exhibited, presented,
Offered, guided, controlled, pitch-perfect,
Full of early morning phrases and framing,
The candlelight swallowed by the sun's first rays,
But still plenty of shadows above and below
And held in every corner.

Nothing pre-negotiated, paid for later
in some other way, maybe while riding
backwards on a goat, or in a dream while
drawing water from a tree with an axe,
or holding up a demon in a flask sealed
with an apple. Never without one.
And maybe with an accomplice or two.

The whole story, or much of it, enough
for your needs. All in its own time,
a corpus of motives peeling back the skin
or reckoned an isolated incident in the tale –
July 18th August 10th? Impossible to determine.
The near repetition kissing back. Whether it is
the predicted or a more exotic corruption of an
already wiredrawn medicinal-mechanical fantasy
annexed to a congruous symmetry, with a subtle
conviction of measure, order, and manner of parts.

A set of essential terms so close to the surface
they're deemed unknowable. Delicate neck, thin
wrists, virginal and pale, surprised and indignant.
Studio, soupente, and roof, with a hand-pump outside
the door. A row of interlocking stone circles just beyond
with smaller circles built in between and a double ring
spun into an extended row of stones reaching the trees.

Some lines of Greek, two women and a man,
the legendary maestro, a parlor, period furniture,
casements, window seat, a piece of chalk, under thatch.

'Azaleas in the sun?' Something's wrong here. He knew
his way around and learned from anything he came across.
From chalk to cheese, from hand and leg. How far?

The quiet, comradely scoff, lacking any malice
briefly succeeds but there are still a lot of empty chairs
plus a reserve of other courtesies to be decided upon.

It's difficult to be thorough in a crowd, but that's the challenge.
You speak quietly to yourself reshaping what you see and hear.
Greetings and transactions. An eye for this an eye for that.

The way back always different from the way there. More
to carry and think about in the lingering words of others.

Manicured to a toothpick.
Some of the parts
had to be left out.

I thought I'd offer what I didn't see already there.
Wrong to imagine anything else.

Rough, thumb-rubbed chiaroscuro—
this is as far into the corners as it will allow.

I remember looking up later and seeing
the afternoon sunlight gold on the snow.

You reached the top by climbing a 130
foot ladder with accomplished grace.

You left early. You didn't run far enough
or fast enough before jumping off the edge.

Now it's too late. But that's your problem
from the start. Only had to learn it once.

You can still turn the page, but it won't
be as easy as before. You're not alone.

Some whiddlewhanging on that flange
if carefully done should get it right again.

He told me and he, this one here, told me.
I didn't need anymore proof. Two's plenty.

Everything comes down to strangers sitting,
spread out on the rail junction's chairs.

They're looking worried, ain't they?
They're from nowhere nearby. One

of them's got red shoes on. I wonder
what that's like. Everybody knows

the train's flooded-out further up the line.
I wonder when they'll find Helen?

At the corner of Dexter and Prospect you see what was meant –
Cat and mouse served to a polished manner, it's quite a show
and always starts overhead; before you look around you have to
look up, quickly at first, and then with growing fascination –
the tongue clicked against the teeth. What will outlast this
 or what could replace it? Apart from the immediate funda-
mental differences, it seems beyond imagining. If you wrote a
story about a man who woke up one day neither tarnished nor
afraid, everything would be overstated and blatant, from the
deep overhang of the roof to what forbidden went on in a grove
of sycamores beyond the hotel.

How many pages taken into the dust?
Fifteen and two drawings. Those in
couplets ascribe a measuring sense, rules—
the rest their application in more or less
credible moments—at home in the dark
instead of the comma'd light of the street.

Consultation and agile choices made, there
will always be things that need to be discussed.
No assurances only deterioration, thereunder
during the aforesaid ashing-over, loess and less.
But it is only natural to want to separate a man
and his words from whatever else he thinks about.

The man, not the writer-servant. Not the traveler
with his highly selective notes to this and that
and the lyric importunings of their effect.
Impracticable but no longer cherished as once.
Anything that could be picked up along the sidewalk
with an enthusiastic but finicky sense of occasion.

Bread 4000 weeks old
everything told and all
withheld one mouthful
or another one morsel
or its parings all parts
of a minoring *this* and
a mirroring *that* with
some success whispered
about its diction and
the querulous domain
of its interiority as suit
an exchange of courtesies
by an enchanted lake or
while enduring some
grudging hospitality
chez Elisabeth Dismal.

An unanticipated intercession –
the machine guessed right

ashamed to speak of it later
–so many Septembers ago

For the missing material and
all that was found in its place

the wind offers conciliatory
terms –disconcerting the rhythm

of things with no adequate name
in the impatient singing silence

Wearing a shoe with a live fox in the toe
while exploring the drifted traces,
something reconciled (after the drum roll)
turns caravan (with a clank) and speeds
with the else-possible mastered in remediation
of haunted ambition and the immediate news
known as the creative act.

Propriety shaped
by inadequacy in
this darkest place –
the drip and
splash – how far
did Atlantis sink?

Somebody's paradise
not just their idea of it.
Palpable and strange,
all the how and why –
with a renewed sense
of the fragile.

Curious convictions
ascribed to pioneers,
I knew they would
come back – and I knew
they would come back
to tell me with an

uncommon sense of
purpose internally achieved –
all of one mind hovering alone
into the glare and
the self-convinced shadows
it achieves and then spares.

A number of syntactical points,
Real, willed, desired, hypothetical—
Aposiopesis interrupts.
The conclusion of a thought is suppressed.

Not certainly known or ascertainable based on
The evidence afforded by the enumeration of implications.
Never declaring the terms of this or that, these or those—
But offering on the fact of some unanswerable choice:

Cross-references are retained in the Accidence
Where various inflections are considered.
Ehem, hues, quoad. Well, hey there, so long as.
Ubinam gentium sumus? Where in the world are we?

These changes are various and complicated.
Any one rendering would be misleading.
Throwing back your head, deponent—passive in form
But active in meaning—thus confrontational—

Your voluntary labor leads you behind a boulder
In the doorway. The blue sky indicates dissatisfaction
With that unlikely number of goat-satyrs playing bagpipes—
An unspoken word from somewhere above.

I'd rather hear you speak than the music play,
A harmony of your scent and cosmology.
It's not good that I haven't seen you in a while.
Shoulders tacitly lifted in doubt—

Intelligent, resourceful, wire-encased,
Reduced to more somber hues.
Any other providing or needing so much
Will be deemed most little praiseworthy nor viable.

Typically a time of violent collisions, a perplexing
Thing about this discovery is that we don't have a
Satisfactory explanation to address what else happened.
Nothing more mysterious than altitude, you might say.

After the scales have been practiced —
Or ambitiously fallen away from the eyes,
A solo doesn't guarantee you have everyone's attention.

Distemper on paper mounted on a lime wood panel.
Older women, their faces heavily rouged and powdered,
And their pale daughters occupied brocaded easy-chairs
That formed two straight lines divided at regular intervals
By long window-curtains of blue and gold velvet and low
Doorways with varnished oak lintels.

They had been materialized and dematerialized
Many times before they got here;
Testing claims, and tracing links, riverine, inconsolable –
Footnotes to mass extinction.
Forgotten, never known, vagrant, still waiting
And the radiant lacking balance

Espousing only something similar –
This contact runs in two directions
Achieving value, losing worth.
A vehicle for ideological and admonitory consent –
See what happens when this is done?
Or this? But by what agency remains a mystery.

Muffled conversations up and down the stairs,
Silence in the room with its cold marble floor.
Physical intelligence and restive attention
Draw together underpinned by taboo to awaken desire.
Tiny pinpricks of light flashed in the dusk –
Diversionary moves. Thus, but not *therefore*.

The pitch of notes fretted on a gonging string
Critical to the ultimate source of mass

Wetting the whistle and whetting the whistle
Fend off fear of loneliness and death

The only thing that has kept us from jumping
Off the cliff is the world and the shame of it

Stay in the wind imagined colder from a warmer room
Warmer if the room be colder

Make any imaginings the *syllables among*
And thus much as you really are

But instead there's nothing from no one
And it's all yours all of it just the chill in the air

At first when the meteor showers began
You met more and more people on the streets
At all times of day eager always to share their
Thoughts prompted by a discrete sense of conjectured
Outcome. And often when three or four had gathered
Shouts of "mine" would be heard–seizing and
Then contriving a moment of personal clarity from
What was a mysterious abundance. But then as
The showers continued day after day and their trajectories
Seemed to alter fewer and fewer people were there to
Encounter and hear bark their claims at the sky
As most now began to take shelter indoors.

WOULD, THE NOTIONAL FIELD

È tutto cosa mia.

Would with a bad name and face pinched.

Striated dispersal—*that* would.

Don't mind if I would.

Plain as would.

The ways wood or wooed would.

Would you ever find anything much better?

What would a colonel say?

What would. What would? What *would?*

Would would. Would would *would.*

Whirling would. [And as whirling would in fell or balmy
  expectation has.]

Would is *that* left ahead in green wood. [Once upon a would.]

Both the wished for and its might are would. Their esperance.

Would wound w-o-u-l-d. And unwound.

Would is enthusing. [Would *then*, perhaps, engage.]

Would can [maybe should] be read horizontally.

The would, be felt.

Would the rhetorhysterical, would the rhetorhistorical.

These and these or those would.

Would, *there* away in hand.

Would–despite no tangible evidence.

Apart from the would of music.

Would as here all these were set–as only I would.

But only in this or that case would.

Would has prospect–but its reach often lacks suspense.

An appetite for risk would.

East of the Black Sea and beyond the Caspian would be the
   Aral Sea.

Would vexes, is invariably suspect.

Would engages, the long answer.

Would considers, the diffuse.

Would conjures the purely informational post apocalyptic.

Would subtly burnished quells.

Would anticipates logical scrutiny.

Would, grievously slow . . . ruminative.

Would, pressed, presses onward.

Would *makes* time and desire from the still invisible erasure.

Would, aching . . .

Would approaches. Over there and over there and over there.
  Would.

Would properly, improperly bantered.

Would-ways advance attribution in light and dark.

Would improves the improvisational.

The button hanging by its single thread would.

Would a distant muffled trumpet make a point here?

Would is the divertimento that is not yet you.

No it would.

Yes it would.

Of course it would—when it would.

The would in the babes and the babes in the would who would.
  Every last one.

A candy butcher would, if anyone remembers.

So much depends on would besides the white chickens.

We could be would.

Had've would.

Would sweeping through.

Would still.

Would from would plus would plus would minus would.

Would to a degree.

Much of the time would.

In and of itself would.

And in a different way would.

Thinner than paper—and would *still*.

Would and a lion in the night.

Werewolves would.

Yes, yes … werewolves would.

All night and into the next day would.

An acre of would and more.

Warren would. Always. And right before he left us would.

Seabrook would Erika would Hannah would Nari would
   Alexis would.

I recall Darylanne would. Though that would be long ago.

We would.

Would in *this* different way, you see.

Would wary, caught up in a slow plunge of desire.

Would despite would.

And would again. Plucking pleasure from necessity.

Seabrook, would Minji, Erika, Hannah, Nari, or Alexis?
  I'd ask you.

Erika, I ask you, would Seabrook or Kendra?

The ould fella would—with any of 'em.

Would's a spiteful maze.

Would *involve*, quite literally . . . Has done so here. *Witness*,
  would.

Would've—as in *has already*. Fate's italics in a mist of emphasis.

Would sure enough.

Would harbingers. Birds calling, wolves howling, the banging
  at doors.

Would of ill omen, its u a sinister smile. Its o an open but
  silenced mouth.

Would's lot.

Would's Lot—sheltered with his daughters.

What would their names be? Not Nari, Hannah, Erika,
  Seabrook, or Alexis.

Or would it?

It would be hard to say.

"Would" whispered in Chinese, French, Arabic, or Italian.

Così sembrerebbe—tuttavia non saprei.

Would would *have*, nevertheless. Nevermore.

And would "in a manner rather rude." [Thanks, Woody.]

Ramified, would demands sacrifices of its secrets.

Would–you get there by stepping stones.

Would–the way back is never the same.

Their would and they're would–and there, *would*.

Would unrestored is would plain and would plane.

Bereft, raw, precarious–would by structure transformed.

Lacking any coherence or permanence apart from would.

Effortless momentum is would and not would.

Would *perfect*, not would-perfect.

Would, in certain circumstances–e.g. if found guilty.

Would is on the air.

Would denied maps.

Storywould.

But would is not *themes continuous* nor is it practical reality

Would, always at a loss.

Would irreducible to data.

The complex frequencies of would determine dimensionality.

Would will betray every compromise with the sacred.

Would begins the argument for the mutation at stake.

Would–it is necessary to overcome this time.

Would–its rigor is always known by another name.

I would and I would and I wouldn't. You and I together. Or I
    alone.

Would–and the sky full of trees turning.

Would?–not if you're looking for immediate information.

Prearranged musical fragments inscribed on inserts and
    arranged in columns inside the box would.

As *that* would, thus–arrowed-up.

The *infinite* defined by the unfinished–that's *all*, and I mean *all*,
    would.

After *what times there are*, what times there would be.

He who wanly entered the world of a Wednesday would.

One Juan would and one Juan would not.

Wouldeuxn't . . . and juandn't–and, of course, wooledn't.

Everywould where–

Would, no penance yet . . .

Would is hang-time.

Would, maybe never once had, until now.

Would across curves, over and under.

Would expects exile, comes from exile.

Would and its estimate –

Would, if a pattern, without a pattern –

Would, always without lexicon –

Would, a million miles distant, a decoy dissolving –

Would in darkness –

Would a diphthong of water and air –

Wouldringing . . .

Werewould . . .

Wouldment . . .

Interruptwould . . . Interrup'twould . . .

Wouldwrack . . .

Rookwould . . .

Wouldiom . . .

Wouldstance . . .

Guesswould . . .

Woëuld . . .

In one direction, waves, sand, sea grass, would.

In another would the waves, would sand, would sea grass?

Would mixing memory and desire?

Carved pillar, humble post, would just the same.

Wouldrings . . .

Wooled and would –

Wouldweller . . .

Wouldust . . .

Would –hypnotic and skeptical . . .

Would –micro, macro, only plural –

Would –eternal marginalia . . .

Would, liminal, unstable, not flat –

Would –allillusion, illillusion –

There is no would-system that explains itself.

Wouldemon . . .

Wouldistant . . .

Wouldoesn't . . . only a matter of time –

Would –wide as a cloud –

Wouldread –

Wouldreach –

Would and the shame of gravity weighed on all sides –

Whittledwould –

Requiring and inward would though would is only outward –

Would on the other side unbridgeable –

Would's temporal continuity is vicissitude.

Would –paraplu- and perfect . . .

Would para, plu, and per*fect* . . .

Would is feline, would is stealth . . .

Would lies in its apparancies.

Would has and has not.

Would would suage –but it cannot. It would not.

Would prodtrays & so . . .

Would's dereliction of assault . . .

And would the quiet assailant –

Would's contemplative subtlety –

Would's deliberative in anticipation of whatever else would.

Wouldnymph, in thine orisons . . .

Would affirms little or nothing.

Would tumbles in the transitive.

Would tosses.

Would + wood + wooed – threaded thus: would comes to 14.

Would has a *feint* echo.

Would is all possible doors and windows.

Wouldruff and wouldrough –

Would = Quasi modo: prima, secunda, tertia, quarta, quinta, sexta, et cetera

Would is aligned by and with the sempiternal.

Would is the semiterminal.

Would looks for a namesake among the antonymic.

Whould –

Whourld –

Would up ahead – 24 hours a day.

Would shapes and reshapes a psychology of the anonymous.

Would, the threat.

Wouldache –

Would's intemperate discontinuity is art.

Woulderama –

Wouldedge –

Wouldwright –

Would –just beyond the discernments of while.

Would picks up where language and music leave off.

Would's fermata.

Wouldid.

Would's horns are valveless.

Would's deviations contain a great deal of information.

Among which would be the 2nd law of thermodynamics.

Would possesses high entropy in its aspect.

There are in would gravitational degrees of freedom in
    anticipation.

Would awaits the particulars.

Would sometimes smiles –but rarely.

There's no squander in would.

Wouldwound, would wound. Wound, wound, and wounder.

Morewould has.

Would lacks tight focus until it's almost too late.

A mean old farmer and a cruel engineer would –and did, says
    Brownie.

A miner for a heart of gold would. And so would I.

These instances and millions like them aptly–neither fully
   expressing nor adorning–would.

Would is a mixture of structure and that which tears structure
   apart.

Would is will mitigated by both has and had.

Would is the logic that approaches through the dimming light.

Would is not often found among the finest turns of speech.

Would eventually.

Would is yet.

Would imparts.

Would never beseecheth.

Would is the arc of the sun and moon.

Would is the path of and in the path of.

Would drifts toward the local when necessary.

Would indifferently bridges fragile domains.

Would introduces every ambition.

Would possesses consistency but lacks patterns of will.

You would even if you wouldn't.

With would all bets are off.

Would in a shaped tone, no filter, no overtones –at first.

Wouldout a doubt.

It'd if only.

Would turns into with a charisma bypass.

Would but only because you cannot.

Though would in another way is wouldn't.

Would to guilt one moment to fear in another.

Would calmly diligent its signature.

A roof and floor of would.

Would waits and whistles.

Would remains unscattered.

Would expects its story, and the rest of it.

Would is what no one tells us.

Would is the cliff.

Would is invisible –then a rain of sparks.

Would after 4 or 5 whiskeys.

Would expands through the next moment before it sets forth.

Would avoids the better instincts of wavelength.

Would is opacity, lack of knowledge leading.

Would the cognitive place or piece of imaginative reality.

Then would come *clog of conscience and sour melancholy.*

Would would have no need of an ascribed coherent sense
   of itself.

Abstract likewise is would's relation to wood and would not.

Would as in "What's next?"

Wouldshod.

And its inverse, wouldshop.

Would wide-ranging, deepening, lingering . . .

Would. *becoming* the slant.

Wouldrites.

Would–in the carving.

Would shapes time.

Would havehashad at once.

Would? How unlikely answered: therefore?

Would greets with virtually no discernible gesture.

No'd. [*With rising inflection*]

As no other blend of time–would.

Would is opportunity–especially for entrapment.

Would in endless variation with neither name nor antecedent.

Proportions would–never clearer than in radical tension.

And they came to Lemnos and would have what they would
have.

However, wouldn't show it. *However* would. In that order.

Would–harsh but graceful.

Would–soon to track the aftermath.

Pernicious would and so would precious–another kind of
pernicious.

Would: *to that extent*, incomplete, rudimentary . . .

Would to which there's an unspecific arbitrariness.

Would, the key turns.

Would, would, would, as would I.

Wouldn't, wouldn't, wouldn't, as would I.

I would, I wouldn't, or not as I would or wouldn't.

Then again who would or wouldn't never matters. It's still,
would?

Would–uncertainty punctuated by nervous laughter.

Would: malicious devotion and resigned anger.

Would, indifferent to all but its own disposition.

Would made outside and abandoned to the darkness it lifts.

Would –well before the previous echoes had.

Predilections and postdilections would.

Would, grained by the coin's milled edge.

Without a doubt the capocosca would.

Would possesses a treacherous intimacy.

When the hurly burly's done, would the battle be lost or won?

Would say: Scopophobia is not the fear of being seen –but the
    fear of being seen *seeing*.

Would is never disturbed by too much waiting.

Would, before it turns into life.

Would, the aperture before the void.

Would, replying incorrectly [fatum].

Would = the space between the space before the space before
    between.

Would of the cross-section.

Would, limited by the next day.

Would under separate names.

Would, the restive ebbing.

Would, by geometrical progressions.

Would, planned then discarded then left to chance.

Would, standing still when completed.

Wouldhatched.

Would doucemalamente, doucemalamente.

Would, noticing nothing.

Would, now so long ago.

Would, though unpersuaded.

Would, never sketched completely.

Would, all in one direction.

Would, rhyming worth with earth.

Would, captive of expectations: no yes and yes . . . no.

Would—stepping away from argumentation.

The stare of would—

Would as ellipsis . . .

Would—inanity, emptiness, dream shadows.

Would, free of flattery.

Would dimensionalizes the virtual.

A pornography of would.

Would—but only until I know.

Would *inside* would.

Would *outside* would–impossible.

But would outside wood is a place to begin.

Would is a trigger of suspense.

Would–need not be persuasive.

Would will always exceed one's vanity.

Would–an isolated agent of action with an invisible subject and
    predicate.

Would–the threat of being given most in what is taken away.

Would is a progress lacking all transcendent pity.

Would–you can't help but stop here . . . but you go on because
    it goes on.

Would: often determined by the difference between pain and
    injury.

Would–with the fatal presence of magic.

Would precedes the rest.

Would, both ceaseless problem and ceaseless solution.

Speculative would–although influence had not yet been exerted.

Would, the proscenium.

Would–beware the paralipsis.

It, would, be: *it would be.*

Would prior to prediction adopts or rejects the purely
mathematical.

Would *enguages*–would engage, would *engaged* with death,
blindness, etc, in no specific order.

Described, epitomized, but unresolved–all would come later
without this set of terms, but another.

Would *enter is would overtake.* [Initially written by hand.]

Endurance and self-assertion as fugue and scherzo would.

Would–patient, obscure, elusive.

Would–like the closed lid on a box.

Claims both vertiginous and parallel are brought to would.

no messages–like a line drawn through–everyone would prefer
to be left alone.

Would eschews the retrocognitive.

Would–you can almost imagine it but you can't quite hear it.

Would is the puppetry of the logarithm.

In a parallel universe 1+1+1+1+1+a+a+a+a+a+b-c would be?

Would levied but unliable–mach theta overcoming accumulated
knowledge.

Wouldluck and wouldlack.

Would in the will of the alluvial.

Would in expectation of a working formula.

If you couldn't fly, swim, sing, chirp, quack, screech, or
talk—what kind of bird would you be?

Would doesn't hunt; would unfolds.

Would—among the misled and those deceived by alignments.

Would above or below not on either side of =.

"We didn't have no capital L so we used an upside down capital
T. We thought it'd work just fine."

Would—a precarious consideration even for the calm and
impartial.

It's raining at the end of the world; and I hear you say without
emphasis: *it would be.*

Never the same after, that is would.

Would: perhaps only an interval . . . a stunted looseness.

You would have me feel the bitter impatience of your
conditional love.

Would at some point must abandon memory, the joint between
space and time.

À l'année prochaine—would only be an estimation.

I would but I know you wouldn't—so how far would we have
come?

Mahakashyapa was absent when the Buddha died, but would
 rush back to supervise the cremation.

As Henry viii had done, Frederick Law Olmsted would marry
 his brother's widow.

Would may never redeem the mind but it makes the mind
 worth redemption.

It'd've done so. Say again? It'd've done so just the same.
 It've –this way or that.

Something leftover from the *Toccata and Fugue in D Minor*
 would do just as well.

He had a variety of tricks, which he would play at random.

Would is inked foliage.

As a page would be tettered with words.

Would miching malicho the paragon.

Nervewould: recovered memory, fanaticism, deviance, and faith.

Would, even so.

The antithesis would be a monolithic resolution –a quintessence
 minus the other 4 essences.

Ancient heirs and dancers would.

Would *and* its common limit.

Would *with* its common limit.

Would ignores nothing and determines what it might.

Would sees wishes and fears through the opposite end of the telescope.

Afterwould.

Would approaching from the future is perceived in the immediate past.

Would and the counterintuitive nature of time.

Would and how soon is right now?

Would expands.

Ply would.

Would is constrained only by what it would.

Would by induction starts to circumscribe.

Would begins with a revised sense of identity.

Privately would remains devoted only to the struggle.

Would is moonlight and moonshine in Moonburgh.

Would–blinking on and off.

Would–lyrical or angular.

Pleasurable longing within a context of finality would.

Would–if nothing else just nature.

Would–the table is set.

Would is the shadow side.

Heard from would? Am now hearing from.

A hatchet with a live snake for a handle would.

Would. Now what?

Would from 60 to 70.

Would—I think you just did.

Would: the partial catalog.

Would the impartial catalog.

Would refigured: would squared.

Would: how much is documentary how much is theater?

Would averted. Now what? More would.

Would by a narrow margin is the wave of the future.

Would and still only halfway there.

Would in the curveship and lends a myth to would.

Would alleges.

Would gathers a few hefty aperçus in the run-up.

Would is the reactive in the suggested option.

Would—the standing wave.
Would holds the mirror.

Would—at the window and the door.

Would despite its common limit, lacking serenity.

Your would, my would, our would –handmade.

Would ahead, clear and away from reunion.

Would –always available to make some point, any point.

Would for a fraction of a second with curious irrelevance.

Would across the shadow of the predator.

Would under the shadow of the prey.

Would awaits its desires.

Would smolders.

New York City, 2012-2013

Other Titles from Otis Books | Seismicity Editions

Erik Anderson, *The Poetics of Trespass*
      Published 2010 | 112 Pages | $12.95
      ISBN-13: 978-0-979-6177-7-5
      ISBN-10: 0-979-6166-7-4

J. Reuben Appelman, *Make Loneliness*
      Published 2008 | 84 pages | $12.95
      ISBN-13: 978-0-9796177-0-6
      ISBN-10: 0-9796177-0-7

Bruce Bégout, *Common Place. The American Motel.*
Translated from the French by Colin Keaveney
      Published 2010 | 143 Pages | $12.95
      ISBN-13: 978-0-979-6177-8-2
      ISBN-10: 0-979-6177-8-

Guy Bennett, *Self-Evident Poems*
      Published 2011 | 96 pages | $12.95
      ISBN-13: 978-0-9845289-0-5
      ISBN-10: 0-9845289-0-3

Guy Bennett and Béatrice Mousli, Editors, *Seeing Los Angeles:
A Different Look at a Different City*
      Published 2007 | 202 pages | $12.95
      ISBN-13: 978-0-9755924-9-6
      ISBN-10: 0-9755924-9-1

Robert Crosson, Signs/ & Signals: *The Daybooks of Robert Crosson*
      Published 2008 | 245 Pages | $14.95
      ISBN: 978-0-9796177-3-7

Robert Crosson, *Daybook* (1983–86)
      Published 2011 | 96 Pages | $12.95
      ISBN-13: 978-0-9845289-1-2
      ISBN-10-9845289-1-1

Mohammed Dib, *Tlemcen or Places of Writing*
Translated from the French by Guy Bennett
      Published 2012 | 120 pages | $12.95
      ISBN-13: 978-0-9845289-7-4
      ISBN-10: 0-9845289-7-0

Ray DiPalma, *The Ancient Use of Stone:*
Journals and Daybooks, 1998–2008
> Published 2009 | 216 pages | $14.95
> ISBN: 978-0-9796177-5-1

Jean-Michel Espitallier, *Espitallier's Theorem*
Translated from the French by Guy Bennett
> Published 2003 | 137 pages | $12.95
> ISBN: 0-9755924-2-4

Forrest Gander, Editor, *Panic Cure: Poems from Spain*
for the 21st Century
> Published 2014 | 304 pages | $12.95
> ISBN: 978-0-9860173-4-6
> ISBN-10: 0-9860173-4-5

Leland Hickman, *Tiresias: The Collected Poems of Leland Hickman*
> Published 2009 | 205 Pages | $14.95
> ISBN: 978-0-9822645-1-5

Michael Joyce, *Twentieth Century Man*
> Published 2014 | 152 Pages | $12.95
> ISBN: 978-0-9860173-2-2

Norman M. Klein, *Freud in Coney Island and Other Tales*
> Published 2006 | 104 pages | $12.95
> ISBN: 0-9755924-6-7

Luxorius, *Opera Omnia or, a Duet for Sitar and Trombone*
Translated from the Latin by Art Beck
> Published 2012 | 216 pages | $12.95
> ISBN-13: 978-0-9845289-6-7
> ISBN-10: 0-9845289-5-4

Ken McCullough, *Left Hand*
> Published 2004 | 191 pages | $12.95
> ISBN: 0-9755924-1-6

Béatrice Mousli, Editor, *Review of Two Worlds:*
French and American Poetry in Translation
> Published 2005 | 148 pages | $12.95
> ISBN: 0-9755924-3-2

Laura Mullen, *Enduring Freedom*
Published 2012 | 80 Pages | $12.95
ISBN-13: 978-0-9845289-8-1
ISBN-10: 0-9845289-8-9

Ryan Murphy, *Down with the Ship*
Published 2006 | 66 pages | $12.95
ISBN: 0-9755924-5-9

Aldo Palazzeschi, *The Arsonist*
Translated from the Italian by Nicholas Benson
Published 2013 | 232 pages | $12.95
ISBN-13: 978-0-9845289-9-8
ISBN: 0-9845289-9-7

Dennis Phillips, *Navigation: Selected Poems, 1985–2010*
Published 2011 | 288 pages | $14.95
ISBN-13: 978-0-9845289-4-3
ISBN-10: 0-9845289-4-6

Antonio Porta, *Piercing the Page: Selected Poems 1958–1989*
Translated from the Italian by Anthony Baldry, Rosemary Leidl, et al
Published 2011 | 368 pages | $14.95
ISBN-13: 978-0-9845289-5-0
ISBN-10: 0-9845289-5-4

Eric Priestley, *For Keeps*
Published 2009 | 264 pages | $12.95
ISBN: 978-0-979-6177-4-4

Sophie Rachmuhl, *A Higher Form of Politics: the Rise of a Poetry Scene, Los Angeles, 1950-1990*
Translated from the French by Mindy Menjou & George Drury Smith
Published 2014 | 352 pages | $12.95
ISBN-13: 978-0-9860173-5-3
ISBN-10: 0-9860173-5-3

Ari Samsky, *The Capricious Critic*
Published 2010 | 240 pages | $12.95
ISBN-13: 978-0-979-177-6-8
ISBN-10: 0-979-6177-6-6

Giovanna Sandri, *only fragments found*
Translated from the Italian by Guy Bennett, Faust Pauluzzi,
and Giovanna Sandri.
> Published 2014 | 336 pages | $14.95
> ISBN-10: 0-9860173-1-0
> ISBN-13: 978-0-9860173-1-5

Hélène Sanguinetti, *Hence This Cradle*
Translated from the French by Ann Cefola
> Published 2007 | 160 pages | $12.95
> ISBN: 970-0-9755924-7-2

Janet Sarbanes, *Army of One*
> Published 2008 | 173 pages | $12.95
> ISBN-13: 978-0-9796177-1-3
> ISBN-10: 0-9796177-1-5

Severo Sarduy, *Beach Birds*
Translated from the Spanish by Suzanne Jill Levine and Carol Maier
> Published 2007 | 182 pages | $12.95
> ISBN: 978-9755924-8-9

Adriano Spatola, *The Porthole*
Translated from the Italian by Beppe Cavatorta and Polly Geller
> Published 2011 | 112 pages | $12.95
> ISBN-13: 978-0-9796177-9-9
> ISBN-10: 0-9796177-9-0

Adriano Spatola, *Toward Total Poetry*
Translated from the Italian by Brendan W. Hennessey and
Guy Bennett,
with an Introduction by Guy Bennett
> Published 2008 | 176 pages | $12.95
> ISBN-13: 978-0-9796177-2-0
> ISBN-10: 0-9796177-3-1

Carol Treadwell, *Spots and Trouble Spots*
> Published 2004 | 176 pages | $12.95
> ISBN: 0-9755924-0-8

Paul Vangelisti, *Wholly Falsetto with People Dancing*
> Published 2013 | 136 pages | $12.95
> ISBN: 978-0-9860173-0-8

Allyssa Wolf, *Vaudeville*
Published 2006 | 82 pages | $12.95
ISBN: 0-9755924-4-0